Ella visited the supermarket with her dad over the weekend.

There were various items displayed at the supermarket.

Ella and her dad were browsing the store together when they noticed some apples.

"Ella, how much is one of these apples?" her dad asked.

"It says $1.50," Ella replied.

"That's right. Do you know what your grandpa farms?" her dad asked.

"Corn."

"How much is corn?"

"There, six for $1.50," Ella said, pointing.

"So, one apple and six ears of corn cost the same?"

"Yes, both are $1.50."

$1..50

There were many items in the market, each with a different price tag. Ella became curious.

"Dad, who decides all these prices?"

"It's the 'invisible hand' that decides," her dad said with a smile.

"The invisible hand?"

"Ella, you like apples, right? You'd want to eat them even if they were $3 each.
But our neighbor John doesn't like apples, so he wouldn't buy them for $3.

Everyone has a different opinion on what they're willing to pay. When the opinions of people who want to buy and the farmers who want to sell match, the price is decided.

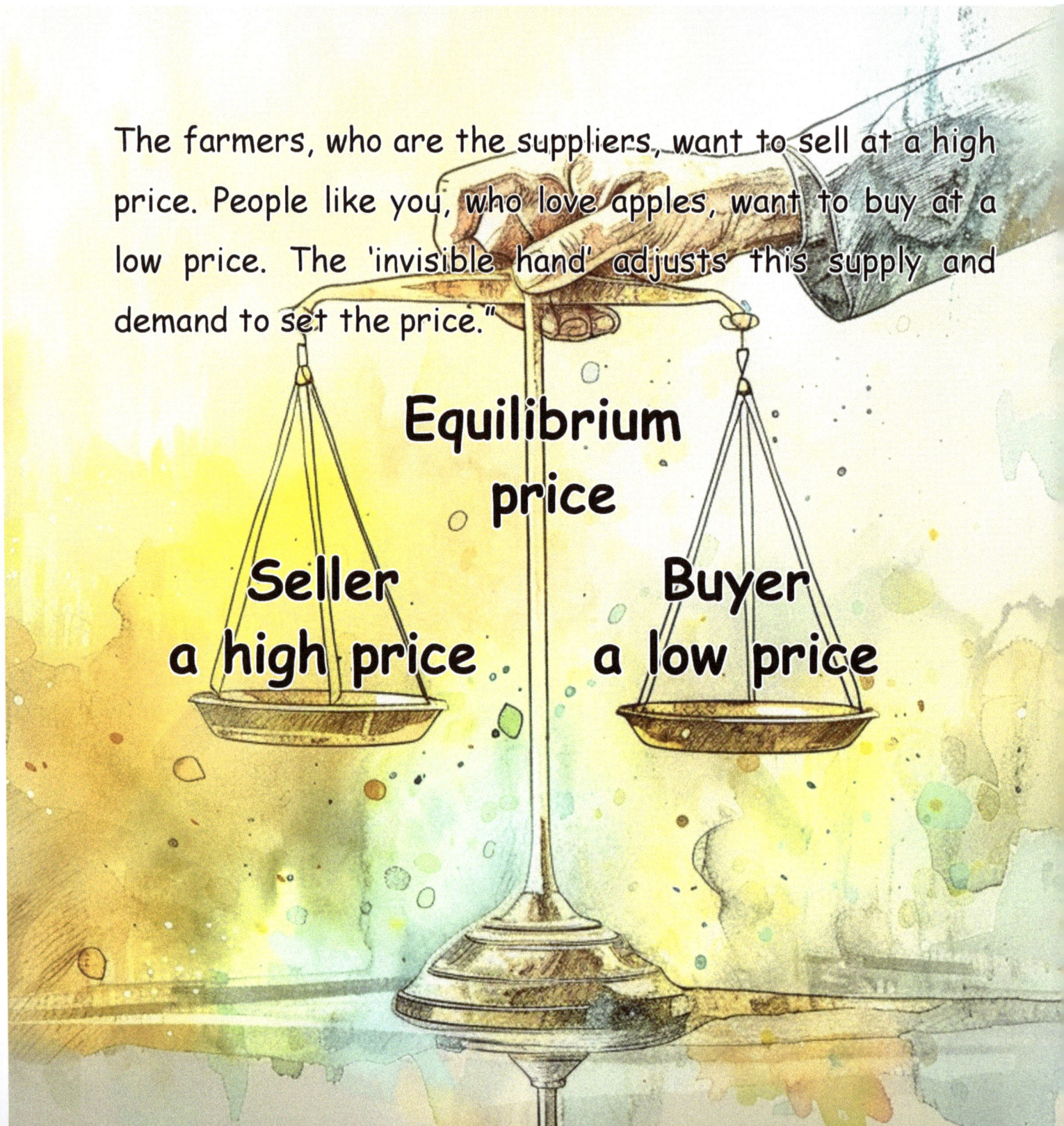
The farmers, who are the suppliers, want to sell at a high price. People like you, who love apples, want to buy at a low price. The 'invisible hand' adjusts this supply and demand to set the price."

Equilibrium price

Seller
a high price

Buyer
a low price

"The 'invisible hand' must be very busy," Ella imagined.

Ella and her dad found the discount corner.

"Dad, here's the discount corner! Why are these apples cheaper?"

SALE

"Well, these apples are a bit older, so they need to be sold quickly. That's why they're cheaper. By using discounts, you can buy items for less."

Ella thought about the importance of money.

"Dad, what if we didn't have money?"

"If we didn't have money, we'd have to trade your grandpa's six ears of corn for the apples. For other items, we'd need a lot more corn. That's why money is so convenient."

"Yes, when I earn a lot of money, I'll buy you something delicious," Ella promised.

Ella and her dad greeted a friendly cashier while finishing their shopping.
Ella smiled, thinking about what she had learned.

Ella and her dad finished their shopping with smiles and went home.

honglee books recommended books

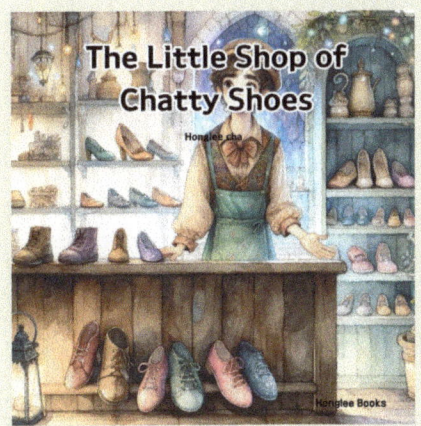
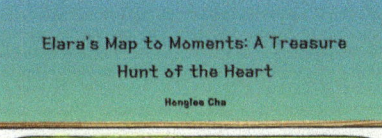

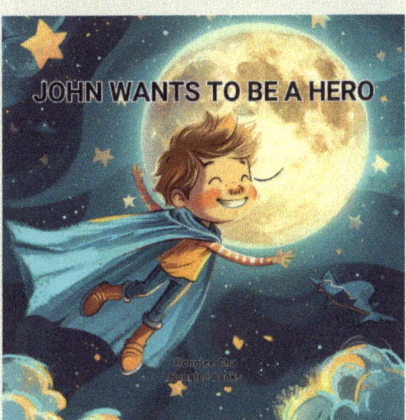
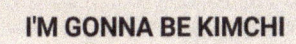

honglee books recommended books

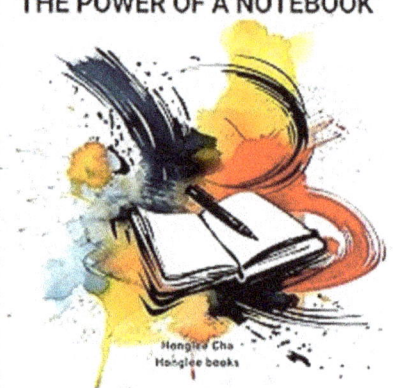

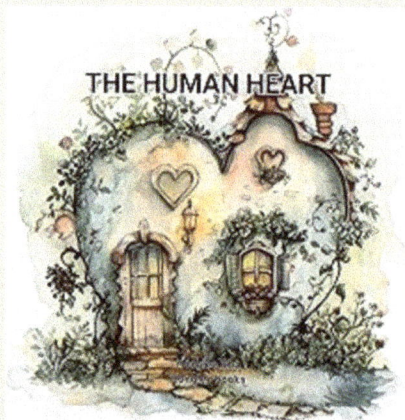

honglee books recommended books

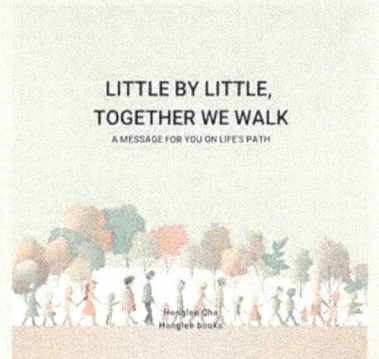

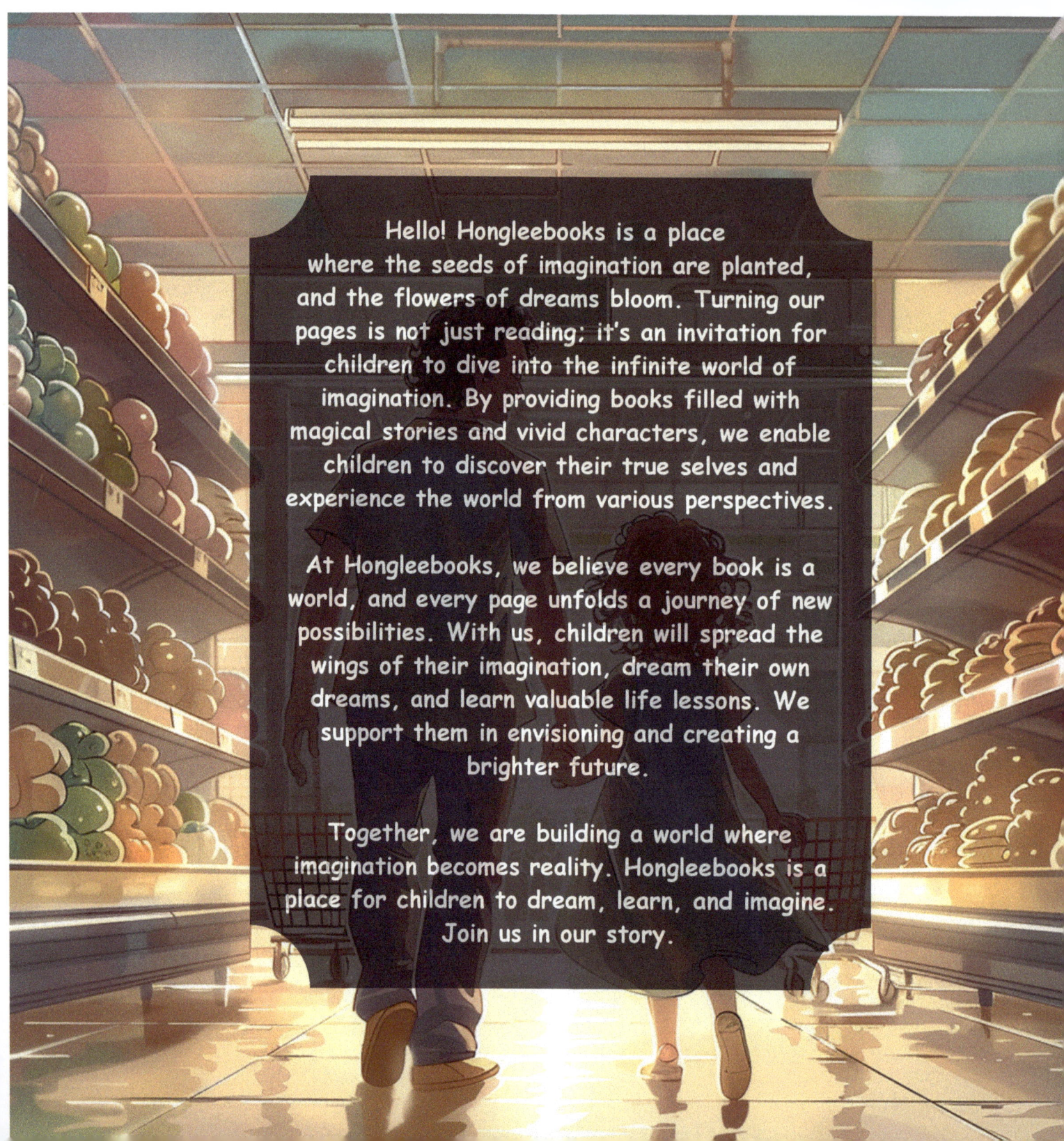

Hello! Hongleebooks is a place where the seeds of imagination are planted, and the flowers of dreams bloom. Turning our pages is not just reading; it's an invitation for children to dive into the infinite world of imagination. By providing books filled with magical stories and vivid characters, we enable children to discover their true selves and experience the world from various perspectives.

At Hongleebooks, we believe every book is a world, and every page unfolds a journey of new possibilities. With us, children will spread the wings of their imagination, dream their own dreams, and learn valuable life lessons. We support them in envisioning and creating a brighter future.

Together, we are building a world where imagination becomes reality. Hongleebooks is a place for children to dream, learn, and imagine. Join us in our story.

www.ingramcontent.com/pod-product-compliance
Lightning Source LLC
LaVergne TN
LVHW072132060526
838201LV00072B/5022